Family Christmas Traditions
Memories, Music, Meals & More
A Keepsake

I0519348

MARYA PATRICE SHERRON

KI PRODUCTIONS

Where every story matters

All rights reserved.

Printed in the United States of America
ISBN: 978-1-961605-25-1

First Edition

Written, Designed, & Edited by Marya Patrice Sherron
Copyright © 2023. All Rights reserved.
No portion of this book may be reproduced, stored in a retrieval
system, or transmitted in any form or by any means, electronic,
mechanical, photocopy, recording, scanning, or others without
permission from the author. If you would like permission to use
material from the book, schedule a reading, recording, or class visit,
please contact: maryapatrice@gmail.com.

Family Christmas Traditions

Memories, Music, Meals & More

A Keepsake

MARYA PATRICE SHERRON

This belongs to

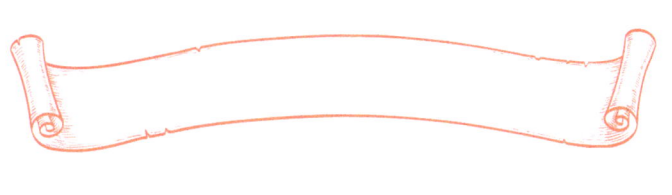

Keepsake Contents

Time to gather recipes...

Collect & write down all the family recipes you can. Be sure to include your personal favorites.

Include all those delicious side-dishes, sweet-treats, and favorite beverages for all ages.

Part I

Family Recipes

Family Favorite Recipe

_____

INGREDIENTS

DIRECTIONS

Family Favorite Recipe

_____

INGREDIENTS

DIRECTIONS

Family Favorite Recipe

INGREDIENTS

DIRECTIONS

Family Dessert Recipe

INGREDIENTS

DIRECTIONS

NOTES

Family Dessert Recipe

_____

INGREDIENTS

DIRECTIONS

NOTES

Family Dessert Recipe

INGREDIENTS

DIRECTIONS

NOTES

Recipe Title

Directions:

Ingredients:

Notes:

Directions:

Ingredients:

SUGAR

Notes:

Directions:

Ingredients:

Notes:

Recipe Title

Directions:

Ingredients:

SUGAR

Notes:

Nostalgia...
Time To Remember

Use this section to record your special memories. Reflect on the Christmases of the past and write what comes to mind.

You will have an opportunity to collect family stories & favorites in the interview section. For now, focus on your own.

Part II
Memories

A Special Memory

When did
this happen?

Written by:

Give it a
fun title...

Childhood Favorites

_____

_____

_____

_____

_____

_____

_____

_____

_____

_____

Jot down all of
your favorites as
a child...
activities, foods,
or places.

Favorite Family Quote

quote by:

_____

Dear Santa,

_____

_____

_____

_____

_____

_____

_____

_____

_____

_____

Write what you can remember about special gifts you wanted and when.

Top 10 Christmas Songs

1

2

3

4

5

6

7

8

9

10

Write down lyrics to a favorite Christmas song.

A Special Memory

When did
this happen?

Written by:

Give it a
fun title...

_____
_____
_____
_____
_____
_____
_____
_____
_____
_____
_____

More Childhood Favorites

_____

_____

_____

_____

_____

_____

_____

_____

_____

_____

Favorite Family Quote

quote by:

_____

Special Decorations

Sketch a favorite decoration or ornament & describe it below.

_____

_____

_____

_____

_____

_____

Let's Play

Use the following pages to record family games & fun traditions.

Have the children in the family write a letter to Santa & have fun gathering superlatives.

Part III

Fun & Games

Family Games

Jot down your favorite family games.

Family Games

Jot down your favorite family games.

Family Superlatives

Best Storytellers

Best Tree

Best Mac & Cheese

Best Jokes

Best Playlist

Best Hair

Best Gift-Giver

Best Dressed

Family Superlatives

Make up a few of your own & ask around.

Best

Best

Best

Best

Best

Best

Best

Best

Family Superlatives

Make up a few of your own & ask around.

Best

Best

Best

Best

Best

Best

Best

Best

Dear Santa,

_____

_____

_____

_____

_____

_____

_____

_____

_____

_____

Time for the kids to write

_____

_____

_____

_____

_____

_____

_____

_____

_____

_____

Dear Santa,

Time for the kids to write

_____

_____

_____

_____

_____

_____

_____

_____

_____

_____

Dear Santa,

_____

_____

_____

_____

_____

_____

_____

_____

_____

Time for the kids to write

_____

_____

_____

_____

_____

_____

_____

_____

_____

_____

_____

Dear Santa,

_____

_____

_____

_____

_____

_____

_____

_____

_____

_____

Time for the kids to write

_____

_____

_____

_____

_____

_____

_____

_____

_____

_____

There's no place like home.

Sounds & Sights of the Season

Music fills homes with joy & laughter during the holiday season. Use the following pages to record your personal & family favorites.

Movies and television shows have become part of many family Christmas traditions. Share yours.

Part IV

Music & Movies

The Sounds of the Season

Top 10 Family Christmas Songs

1

2

3

4

5

6

7

8

9

10

Write down lyrics to a favorite Christmas song.

Favorite Christmas Movies

1 _____

2 _____

3 _____

Favorite Christmas T.V. Shows

1 _____

2 _____

3 _____

Family Favorite Christmas Movies

1 _____

2 _____

3 _____

Family Favorite Christmas T.V. Shows

1 _____

2 _____

3 _____

Meaning & Remembrance

Use this section to delve into the meaning of Christmas for you & your family.

Space is provided to name & remember your deceased loved ones. Share a memorable story or write as you are so moved.

Part V
The Meaning of Christmas

Use the next few pages
to describe the special
ways your family
celebrates the true
meaning of Christmas.

In Honor of Those No Longer With Us.

In Loving Memory of:

_____

In Loving Memory of:

_____

In Loving Memory of:

_____

In Loving Memory of:

_____

The Gift of Family Stories

This section is all about preserving traditions and documenting family stories. Use the following pages to interview as many as possible.

Have fun and be creative — there are many ways to gather stories. This is a keepsake you can pass along for generations. Fill the pages with the riches of your family.

Part VI
Family Interviews

A Special Memory

Told by:

Written by:

_____

_____

_____

_____

_____

_____

_____

_____

_____

_____

Favorite Dessert

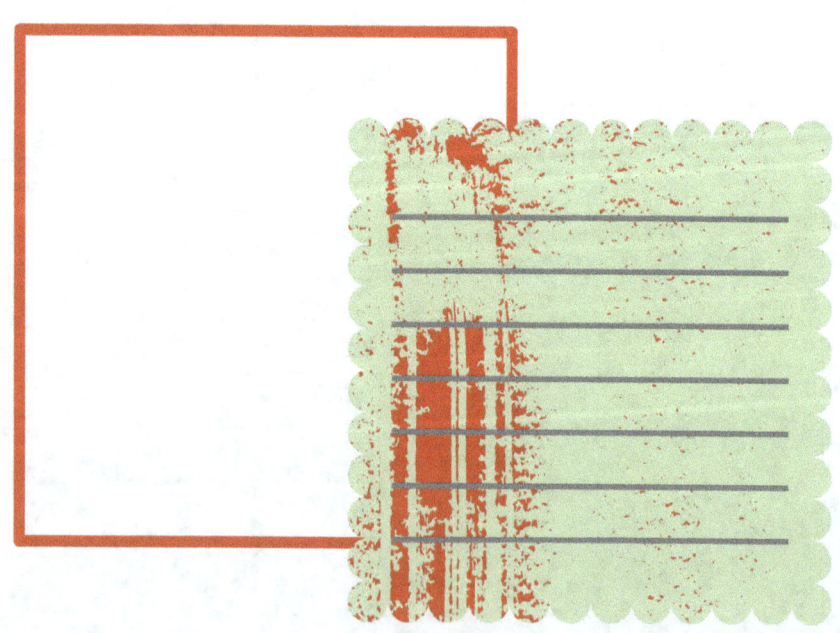

Special Decorations

Sketch a favorite decoration or ornament & describe it below.

_____
_____
_____
_____
_____
_____

Childhood Favorites

_____

_____

_____

_____

_____

_____

_____

_____

_____

_____

Jot down all of
your favorites as
a child...
activities, foods,
or places.

Favorite Family Quotes

quote by:

_____

favorite of:

_____

A Special Memory

When did
this happen?

Written by:

Give it a
fun title...

Favorite Dessert

Special Decorations

Sketch a favorite decoration or ornament & describe it below.

Childhood Favorites

_____

_____

_____

_____

_____

_____

_____

_____

_____

_____

Jot down all of
your favorites as
a child...
activities, foods,
or places.

Favorite Family Quotes

quote by:

_____

favorite of:

_____

A Special Memory

When did
this happen?

Written by:

Give it a
fun title...

_____
_____
_____
_____
_____
_____
_____
_____
_____

Favorite Dessert

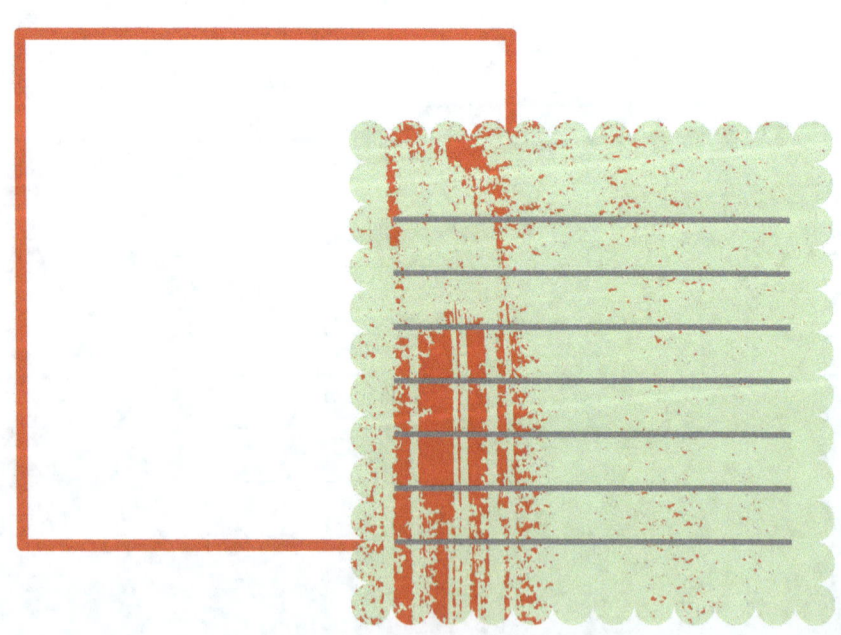

Special Decorations

Sketch a favorite decoration or ornament & describe it below.

_____

_____

_____

_____

_____

Childhood Favorites

_____

_____

_____

_____

_____

_____

_____

_____

_____

_____

Jot down all of
your favorites as
a child...
activities, foods,
or places.

Favorite Family Quotes

quote by:

_____

favorite of:

_____

A Special Memory

When did
this happen?

Written by:

Give it a
fun title...

_____

_____

_____

_____

_____

_____

_____

_____

_____

_____

Favorite Dessert

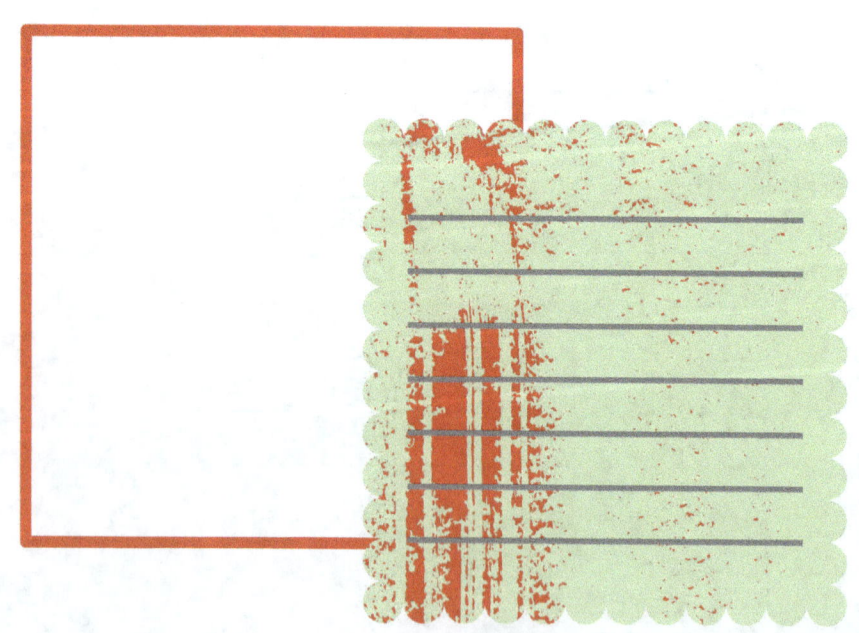

Special Decorations

Sketch a favorite decoration or ornament & describe it below.

Childhood Favorites

_____

_____

_____

_____

_____

_____

_____

_____

_____

_____

Jot down all of
your favorites as
a child...
activities, foods,
or places.

Favorite Family Quotes

quote by:

_____

favorite of:

_____

A Special Memory

When did
this happen?

Written by:

Give it a
fun title...

_____
_____
_____
_____
_____
_____
_____
_____
_____
_____

Favorite Dessert

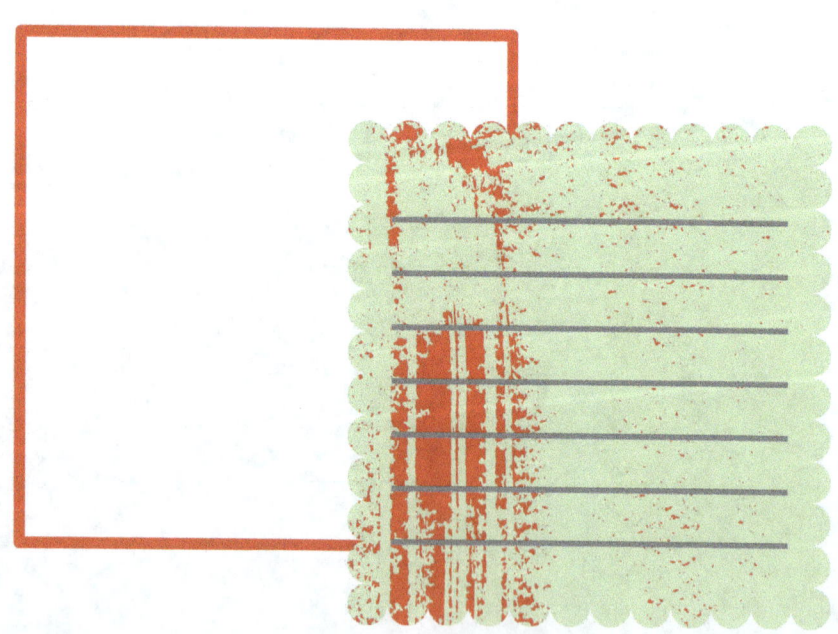

Special Decorations

Sketch a favorite decoration or ornament & describe it below.

Childhood Favorites

_____

_____

_____

_____

_____

_____

_____

_____

_____

_____

Jot down all of
your favorites as
a child...
activities, foods,
or places.

Favorite Family Quotes

quote by:

_____

favorite of:

_____

A Special Memory

When did
this happen?

Written by:

Give it a
fun title...

Favorite Dessert

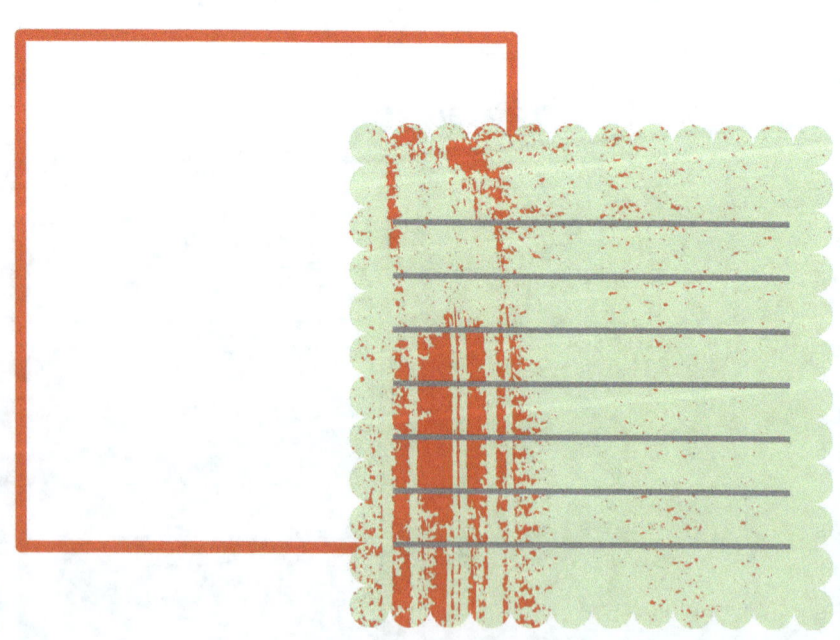

Special Decorations

Sketch a favorite decoration or ornament & describe it below.

Childhood Favorites

_____

_____

_____

_____

_____

_____

_____

_____

_____

_____

Jot down all of
your favorites as
a child...
activities, foods,
or places.

Favorite Family Quotes

quote by:

_____

favorite of:

_____

A Special Memory

When did
this happen?

Written by:

Give it a
fun title...

_____
_____
_____
_____
_____
_____
_____
_____
_____
_____

Favorite Dessert

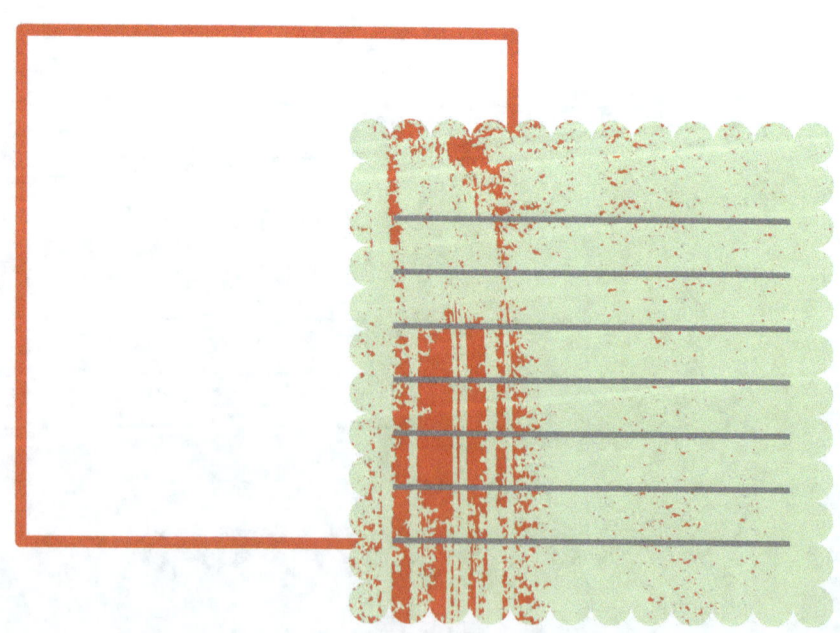

Special Decorations

Sketch a favorite decoration or ornament & describe it below.

_____

_____

_____

_____

_____

Childhood Favorites

_____

_____

_____

_____

_____

_____

_____

_____

_____

_____

Jot down all of
your favorites as
a child...
activities, foods,
or places.

Favorite Family Quotes

quote by:

_____

favorite of:

_____

A Special Memory

When did
this happen?

Written by:

Give it a
fun title...

_____

_____

_____

_____

_____

_____

_____

_____

_____

_____

_____

Favorite Dessert

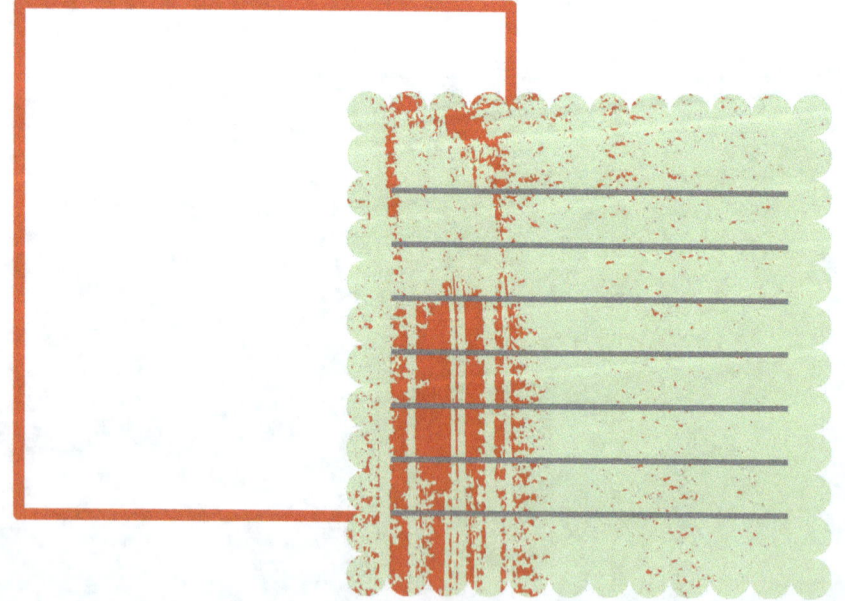

Special Decorations

Sketch a favorite decoration or ornament & describe it below.

Childhood Favorites

_____

_____

_____

_____

_____

_____

_____

_____

_____

_____

Jot down all of your favorites as a child... activities, foods, or places.

Favorite Family Quotes

quote by:

_____

favorite of:

_____

So much to do...

Use this section to help you plan for the holidays.

Brainstorm gift ideas, plan your menu & stay organized.

Part VII
Holiday Planning

to-do list

- [ ]
- [ ]
- [ ]
- [ ]
- [ ]
- [ ]
- [ ]
- [ ]
- [ ]
- [ ]
- [ ]
- [ ]

to-do list

- ☐
- ☐
- ☐
- ☐
- ☐
- ☐
- ☐
- ☐
- ☐
- ☐
- ☐
- ☐

Gift Ideas for...

- ●
- ●
- ●
- ●
- ●
- ●
- ●

Gift Ideas for...

- ○ ....
- ○ ....
- ○ ....
- ○ ....
- ○ ....
- ○ ....
- ○ ....

Gift Ideas for...

-
-
-
-
-
-
-

Gift Ideas for...

Gift Ideas for...

- _____
- _____
- _____
- _____
- _____
- _____
- _____

Self-Care Gems

Holidays can be a stressful time. Ask family members what they do to stay calm, well-rested, and enjoy time with family.

by:

by:

by:

by:

Self-Care Gems

by:

by:

by:

by:

What's on the Menu?

- [ ]
- [ ]
- [ ]
- [ ]
- [ ]
- [ ]
- [ ]
- [ ]
- [ ]
- [ ]
- [ ]
- [ ]

Space for You

Use the following pages to respond to some or all of the writing prompts... or write freely.

Think about any special details or unique traditions that you want to add.

Part VIII
Writing Prompts

Prompts to Consider

What does Christmas mean to you?

What family traditions do you hope will remain?

Do you have complex feelings around the holidays? For example, joy but also sadness due to loss.

Describe your ideal Christmas Day.

Where is a place you would like to celebrate Christmas that you haven't already?

Describe other favorite Christmas traditions and activities like plays, making ornaments, or Christmas caroling.

Describe challenges that accompany the holiday season.

Have you witnessed a Christmas miracle? Tell your story.

_____

_____

_____

_____

_____

_____

_____

_____

_____

_____

_____

_____

_____

_____

_____

_____

_____

_____

_____

_____

_____

_____

_____

_____

_____

_____

_____

_____

_____

_____

_____

It all began...

One Silent Night.

www.ingramcontent.com/pod-product-compliance
Lightning Source LLC
Chambersburg PA
CBHW071404120626
46546CB00002B/806